Suzuki Piano School
Volume 7
Revised Edition

CONTENTS

About This Edition

The notes and performance indications (dynamics, articulation, phrasing, pedalings and ornaments) of this edition correspond with authenticated Urtext sources.

Additional markings are identified as "editorial" by use of parentheses and broken lines (slurs). All fingerings are editorial.

© 1992, 1973, 1972 Dr. Shinichi Suzuki
Sole publisher for the entire world except Japan:
Summy-Birchard Inc.
exclusively distributed by
Warner Bros. Publications
15800 N.W. 48th Avenue, Miami, Florida 33014
All rights reserved   Printed in U.S.A.

ISBN 0-87487-444-0

The Suzuki name, logo and wheel device
are trademarks of Dr. Shinichi Suzuki used
under exclusive license by Summy-Birchard, Inc.

1 Sonata

W.A. Mozart
K331
Published in Vienna, 1784

Andante grazioso

Var. I

4

Var. III

Var. V
Adagio

12

Menuetto

14

TRIO

(Menuetto D.C.)

ALLA TURCA
Allegretto

2 Prelude

G.F. Händel
From Suite No. 14 in G Major, Allegro